HER.
GUIDED JOURNAL

OTHER BOOKS BY
Pierre Alex Jeanty

Best Sellers

HER.

HER Vol. 2

Unspoken Feelings of a Gentleman

To the Women I Once Loved

Other Books

Unspoken Feelings of a Gentleman 2

In Love With You

Apologies That Never Came

Really Moving On

Sparking Her Own Flame

Watering Your Soil

Free Downloads

Watering Your Soil
Download at www.wateringyoursoil.com

Copyright © 2021 by Pierre Alex Jeanty

All rights reserved. No part of this publication may be reproduced, stored in a retrieval system, or transmitted tin any form or by any means - electronic, mechanical, photocopying, recording, or otherwise - without the written permission of the publisher.

Graphic Design & Layout: Patti Brassard Jefferson

ISBN: 978-1-949191-14-1

For more information, please visit:
PierreJeanty.com
Contact: Pierre@PierreAlexJeanty.com

Acknowledgements

I want to acknowledge you
for working on YOU.
It isn't always easy to make that decision.
These pages are dedicated to a better you.

To Patti Jefferson,
Thank you for helping this vision of mine
become a reality.

To you...

Thank you for allowing my words
to come into your world.

If you have this journal, chances are you've read
HER and HER Vol. 2. If you haven't yet,
please make sure you grab them.
This journal is meant to flow with them.

When putting your thoughts in this journal...
Be raw.
Be honest with yourself.
Be an open book pouring into these pages.
This is how you will see the power
in this beautiful project my team and I
put together for you.

Enjoy it.

— Pierre

Some things to look for in the book...

Write a letter

Letter prompts are designed to help you figure out what you really need to put into words so that you can free up space in your head — and heart — for more positive things.

Write what's on your mind

This is space for you to write whatever you want. What's on your heart, your accomplishments, your grievances, silliness, dreams, goals, or disappointments. Journal about your day, your life, or your relationships. Date your entries and revisit them when you need to see where you were or remind yourself of where you are going.

Respond to questions

The questions are posed to make you think past your comfort level. There is no audience to judge your answers so it is safe to be honest. You deserve that from you.

Make a list

The lists that you generate can be used as tools to help you navigate the next steps in your healing or growth. Having bullet point summaries of your experiences, lessons, and goals will help you stay focused and can be used as your personal checklists.

Self-love affirmations

Positive affirmations are phrases or mantras that you repeat on a regular basis which describe who you want to be or a particular end result you wish to achieve. Reciting them regularly will lead your subconscious mind to believe them. Even if you don't believe them in the beginning, they will eventually become your reality.

5 Five word poems

Write a poem and incorporate the five words given. That's really the only rule. Stretch yourself and embrace your creativity.

It's time to get started...

You are BECOMING.

Allow yourself to be who you need to be.

Date: _____

POETRY PROMPT

Who do you see yourself becoming?

What does it mean to you to "become you"?

 *List the things that currently make you smile.*

_____

_____

_____

_____

_____

List your favorite things about yourself.

_____

_____

_____

_____

_____

When do I feel strong?

What makes me strong?

Date: _____

Confidence looks amazing on you!

Date: _____

You should like who you are becoming.

I ACKNOWLEDGE I AM MORE THAN ENOUGH.

♥

I AM COMMITTED TO MY GROWTH.

♥

I AM CONSTANTLY IMPROVING.

♥

TODAY, I AM ONE STEP CLOSER TO MY DREAMS.

♥

I AM READY TO EMBRACE MY TRUE SELF.

♥

I RECOGNIZE THAT I AM ON THE RIGHT PATH.

FLUTTER   **WINDOW**
          MORNING
TRANSFORM   **COCOON**

5

Date: _____

Define yourself. That's no one else's job.

Date: _____

Your story is yours. You can own it or change it.

Date: _____

Who I am today...

Me in 6 months...

My poem about the differences:

POETRY PROMPT

Date: _____

Write about that one really embarrassing moment you had...

Did you survive? ❏ *Yes* ❏ *Of course*

 *List the habits you are trying to let go.*

 *The habits I was happiest to get rid of ...*

What happened when I did...

Date: _____

Don't let the ghosts of your past...

Date: _____

...scare the life out of your new relationships.

I AM AT PEACE WITH MY PAST AND READY TO MOVE FORWARD.

♥

I FORGIVE MYSELF FOR MY MISTAKES AND LEARN FROM THEM.

♥

MY FUTURE IS BRIGHT AND I DESERVE IT.

♥

I AM NOT DEFINED BY THE FAILURES OF MY PAST.

♥

I AM WORTHY OF MY OWN PATIENCE.

♥

I AM FOCUSED ON MY NOW.

BUNDLE　　　　　　　　　　**FAIL**
　　　　　AWAKEN
CLOCK　　　　　　　　　　**SLUMBER**

5

Date: _____

Today isn't yesterday...

Date: _____

...and you aren't who you were.

She is a **MERMAID** going against the flow

Date: _____

What direction are things flowing in your life?

_____
_____

Your work?

_____
_____
_____

Family?

_____
_____
_____

Relationships?

_____
_____
_____

Date: _____

Things I should do against the flow...

The consequences...

Date: _____

POETRY PROMPT
Going with the flow is easy. Going against the flow takes courage.

Date: _____

The wave society expects you to follow...

Date: _____

...may drown your true identity.

I SEE OPPORTUNITY WHERE OTHERS SEE CHALLENGES.

♥

I AM READY TO SEE THINGS DIFFERENTLY.

♥

I HOLD THE POWER TO CHOOSE MY DESTINY.

♥

I CANNOT EXPEND ENERGY ON THINGS I CAN NOT CONTROL.

♥

MY COMFORT ZONE SETS BARRIERS I NEED TO LET GO.

♥

I TRUST MY INTUITION TO MAKE GOOD CHOICES FOR MYSELF.

BUBBLE   SWIRL   VACATION
SAND   MIRROR

5

Date: _____

You can only make waves by going against the tide.

Date: _____

Standing still is easy but it stagnates your soul.

Being NORMAL is over-praised.

You were never meant to be accepted by all.

Therefore, be as  and as  as you want to be.

Date: _____

What are some weird things about you?

Pssst: this is really just a list of your secret super powers! Look how amazing you are!

Most of us feel different and weird as children. Write a letter to your 12-year-old self and let her know how to deal with those feelings.

Hey, this is good advice! Perhaps your today self should listen and embrace those special things that make you weird and different and odd. You aren't twelve anymore and big girls should take pride in their uniqueness.
You are a star. Time to shine!

Date: _____

Be normal, or don't, but always be truly you.

Date: _____

Let others be normal. You be you.

I AM COMFORTABLE WITH MY UNIQUENESS.

♥

I AM AMAZINGLY DIFFERENT.

♥

MY DECISIONS ARE MY OWN AND CAN NOT BE COMPARED TO SOMEONE ELSE'S.

♥

I AM NOT LIKE ANYONE ELSE AND I AM COMFORTABLE WITH THAT.

♥

I FIT IN BEST IN HEALTHY SITUATIONS & WITH POSITIVE PEOPLE.

♥

I GIVE MYSELF PERMISSION TO BE GENUINELY HAPPY.

FANTASY   REALITY
                    ART
ANIMATE   SPLASH

5

Date: _____

Their normal doesn't have to be yours.

Date: _____

Find a way to be yourself.

Beautiful flowers can't bloom without healthy roots.

Date: _____

What/who keeps you rooted in a healthy way?

What/who doesn't keep you rooted in a healthy way?

Go on, color it in if you want to. You don't need permission. It's YOUR book.

 *List some changes you need to make in order to have healthier roots...*

Your roots may need some tending but be confident that you have the right tools to grow yourself into the beautiful flower you were meant to be. Start checking things off the list. You've got this!

POETRY PROMPT

If the grass looks greener on the other side, Stop staring. Stop comparing. Stop complaining and start watering the grass you're standing on.

Date: _____

Date: _____

You are meant to grow and evolve.

Date: _____

Let discomfort push you toward growth.

I AM COMMITTED TO MY GROWTH.

♥

I CAN START MY GROWTH WITH SMALL STEPS. I WILL TAKE LARGER STEPS WHEN I AM ABLE.

♥

I AM OPEN TO NEW EXPERIENCES, PEOPLE, AND OUTCOMES.

♥

I AM TEACHABLE AND OPEN TO LEARNING NEW THINGS.

♥

I ACCEPT MY FORWARD MOTION EVEN WHEN SLOW. PROGRESS DOESN'T HAVE A TIME LIMIT.

♥

I AM NOT WHO I WAS YESTERDAY & I CAN SAY THAT TOMORROW, TOO.

BLOSSOM   **SHADE**   **SUNSHINE**

SHOVEL   **BIRD**

5

Date: _____

Flowers grow toward the sun. Step into the light.

Date: _____

Growth can be scary. Not growing is worse.

The mistake of many is that they think **FOREVER** is a **PATH** rather than a **ROAD** that must be built brick by brick.

Date: _____

What is your definition of "forever"?

What doesn't fall under that definition for you?

Date: _____

Make a list of the times you've built PATHS *rather than* ROADS:

These are the paths you've created in the past. Leave them there. When you are ready to start laying bricks, the road will be clear to you.

Date: _____

Date: _____

Strong foundations are built one brick at a time.

Date: _____

Patience is the strongest building material.

Loving myself makes it easier for others to love me.

♥

I am in charge of building my life the way I want it to be.

♥

I do not need to walk an old path if it no longer takes me where I desire to be.

♥

My Forever can start over today. I make the rules.

♥

Crawl. Walk. Run. I've got this!

♥

I can create the life I deserve.

CONCRETE **HOUSE** **AMAZING**

BUILD **SOFT**

Date: _____

Bricks can build walls or roads. You choose.

Date: _____

One step, one day, one brick at a time.

Don't dare her to be **DIFFERENT** she already is.

Dare her to be **HERSELF,**

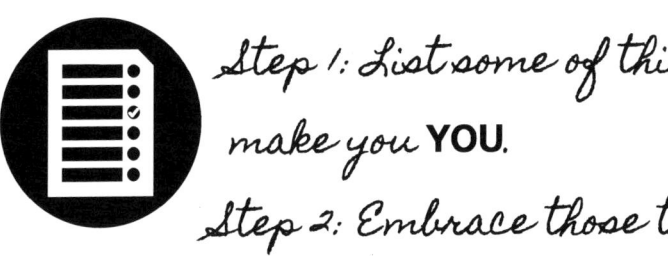

Step 1: List some of things that make you **YOU**.

Step 2: Embrace those things!.

Step 3: Refuse to settle for a partner that doesn't embrace and support you celebrating the very elements that make you who you are.

Date: _____

POETRY PROMPT

Being myself means...

Date: _____

Date: _____

What makes you proud of yourself?

What have you done lately just for you?

What do you need more of in your life?

Date: _____

Don't depend on someone else to tell you who you are.

Date: _____

BEing yourself happens when you BElieve in yourself.

I TRUST MYSELF AND HAVE MY BACK.

♥

MY LIFE WILL CHANGE WHEN I DO.

♥

I WILL NOT MOLD MYSELF TO FIT SOMEONE ELSE'S PERCEPTION OF ME. I AM ENOUGH AS I AM.

♥

I AM IN CHARGE.

♥

I DON'T NEED PERMISSION FROM ANYONE TO BE A HAPPIER ME.

♥

EVERYTHING I WANT TO BE, I ALREADY AM.

ANIMATE

SIZZLE

CANVAS

SOCIAL

CONFETTI

5

Date: _____

Remember, different doesn't mean wrong.

Date: _____

Being different is less scary than being the same.

the sun rises behind her **smile**

And the sunset is in her **Eyes.**

POETRY PROMPT

Sit at the feet of gratitude today & let it help your eyes find beauty in the day.

Date: _____

Date: _____

List 5 things you are grateful for.

_____
_____
_____
_____
_____
_____
_____
_____
_____
_____
_____
_____
_____
_____
_____

List 5 ways you express gratitude.

_____
_____
_____
_____
_____
_____
_____
_____
_____
_____
_____
_____
_____
_____
_____

Date: _____

What are you most grateful for in your life today and why?

No matter your current situation, there is always something in your life to be grateful for. Embracing that gratitude just might make the challenges you are facing easier to deal with.

Date: _____

You are the sun, sweetheart...

Date: _____

...even on cloudy days, you are made to shine!

I AM NOT AFRAID TO SHINE. MY LIGHT IS VALUABLE.

♥

I AM WRAPPED IN LIGHT AND LOVE AND SHARE THAT WITH OTHERS.

♥

I CHOOSE MY OWN PATH.

♥

I AM A BEAUTIFUL EXPRESSION OF LOVE.

♥

I AM EXACTLY WHO I NEED TO BE AT THIS MOMENT.

♥

ALL IS WELL IN MY WORLD AND I AM OKAY WHERE I AM. FOR NOW.

DAWN   INTENSIFY
    BEACH
IMAGINE   THROAT

Date: _____

In her smile lives the light...

Date: _____

...and the darkness of the night sky.

POETRY PROMPT

Loving yourself first is only a pre-requisite of healthy love…

Date: _____

We've all written letters apologizing for regrettable actions or deeds at some point. Let's twist that. Write yourself a letter giving you permission to be unapologetic in your growth or journey.

Date: _____

Now that you have written these words, reread them. Often. Remind yourself that you don't need to apologize, downplay, or diminish your goals, successes, or quirky traits. You deserve someone who respects and honors everything that makes you authentically you. Period.

Date: _____

Keep rising up until you can fly.

Date: _____

Love knows your name.

I AM A UNIQUE GIFT TO THE WORLD.

♥

I DO NOT NEED TO COMPARE MYSELF TO OTHERS. LIFE IS NOT A COMPETITION.

♥

I AM AUTHENTIC.

♥

I DO NOT NEED TO APOLOGIZE FOR BEING MYSELF.

♥

I LOVE AND ACCEPT MYSELF WITH COMPASSION.

♥

I AM CAPABLE OF ACCEPTING MY TRUE SELF.

STIMULATE **BLAME** **PURPLE**
ORCHID **FANFARE**

Date: _____

You owe no one an explanation for being yourself.

Date: _____

You deserve better from you!

The man for you
will understand
that you are
both a
SURVIVOR
and a
WARRIOR,
full of scars, yet
FEARLESS.

Date: _____

What makes me fearful?

When do I feel fearless?

Date: _____

My scars: | *What I learned from them:*

Date: _____

POETRY PROMPT

Love hard, despite how hard it is.

Date: _____

Love is for those who know how to hang on & fight...

Date: _____

... until their arms can't lift themselves anymore.

I WILL NOT BOW TO MY FEARS.

♥

I AM PREPARED FOR TODAY'S CHALLENGES.

♥

I CAN NOT DO THE IMPOSSIBLE AND I DON'T HAVE TO.

♥

DOING THINGS DIFFERENTLY, WILL GIVE ME DIFFERENT OUTCOMES. I AM READY.

♥

I AM COURAGEOUS AND VOW TO STAND UP FOR MYSELF.

♥

I CAN GET THROUGH THIS. I AM AN INDESTRUCTIBLE FORCE.

COMPETE

TRANSFER

APPROVAL

FIGHT

DISTANCE

Date: _____

She isn't meant to be handled with caution...

Date: _____

...but to be loved hard.

You are made of love.
How can you let anyone convince
you that you are not worthy of it?

POETRY PROMPT

Write a letter to a friend going through a hard time with their relationship. What advice can you give them to be resilient and reassure them they will be okay in the end?

Date: _____

Great advice! Of course, you know that you are the friend, right? Read this letter again anytime you need advice from that one person who genuinely cares for you... you!

Date: _____

Only real love can afford you...

Date: _____

...because you are both love and priceless.

I GET TO PICK, AND TODAY I CHOOSE HAPPINESS.

♥

I AM OPEN TO THE GOODNESS THAT I HAVE EARNED.

♥

LOVE KNOWS MY NAME.

♥

I TRUST THAT EVERYTHING WILL BE OKAY.

♥

MY LIFE IS FULL OF PROMISE AND PASSION.

♥

I FORGIVE MYSELF SO THAT I CAN FORGIVE OTHERS.

MOUNTAIN

        GRACE

MATE

SIZZLE

        SQUEEZING

Date: _____

Despite, love is still worth it!

Date: _____

Love should not cost you your sanity.

She is a lioness, with a wild heart and a strong mind.

My lioness traits

Wild heart

Strong mind

Date: _____

What are your personal thoughts on these two statements and how do they apply to you currently?

Strong women not compare themselves to others or put others down to make themselves look better.

Strong women not shrink themselves for the comfort of others.

If you don't feel that they apply to you right now, think about what steps you can take to make sure you are adding mental strength to your growth plans.

Date: _____

Fire burns in her bones, while love flows through her veins.

Poetry Prompt

Date: _____

Date: _____

She is tender and imminent...

Date: _____

... yet tough and full of fire.

I DO NOT ALWAYS HAVE TO BE FIERCE AND STRONG.

♥

I AM A CALMING INFLUENCE TO MYSELF AND OTHERS.

♥

I AM DOING THE BEST I CAN AND THAT IS ENOUGH.

♥

I WILL FACE THE DAY WITH LOVE AND COURAGE.

♥

I DO NOT NEED TO BE TAMED BY ANYONE. MY WILDNESS SUITS ME.

♥

I WILL MAKE TIME FOR MYSELF.

GROWL

TREES

SCARED

WANDER

HERD

5

Date: _____

She did not choose to be alone...

Date: _____

...she simply chose to love herself more.

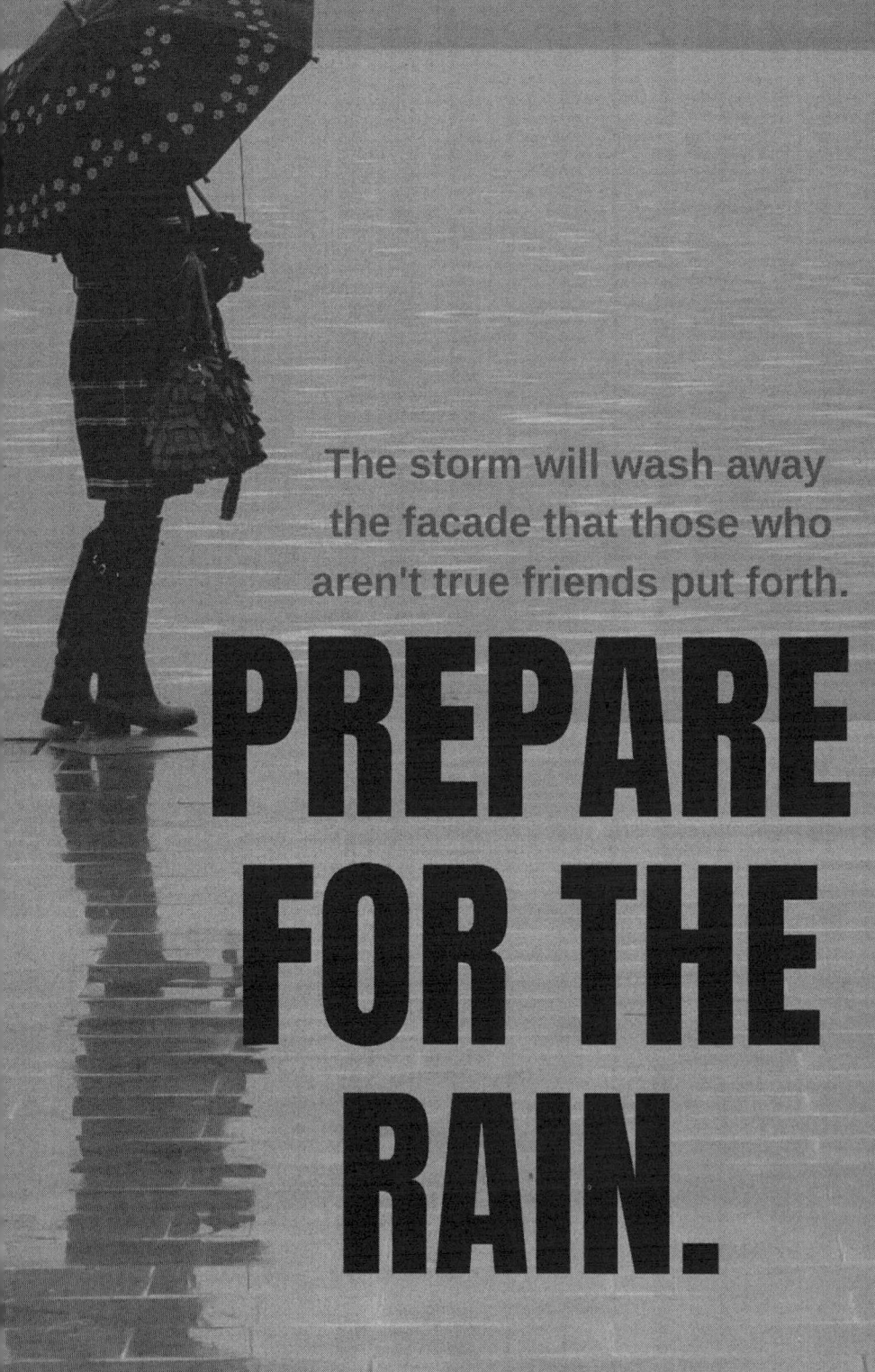

In letting in the opinions
of those who only see a glimpse of
what's in your mirror,
we force ourselves to be things
we aren't born to be.

Date: _____

People will always have something to say about you. Ask yourself this:

What have those people contributed to your life?

Why should what they say carry more meaning than your truth, considering you've been the only one present in your life since day one?

Date: _____

Date:

Things I look for in true friends

Things that make me a true friend

Things that I can do to better align those 2 lists

Date: _____

Their compliments should not define you...

Date: _____

...nor should their criticism break you.

I AM RESPONSIBLE FOR MYSELF.

♥

THE ONLY OPINION OF ME THAT I NEED IS MY OWN.

♥

I DO NOT NEED TO PRETEND TO BE SOMEONE ELSE SO THAT PEOPLE LIKE ME. I AM LIKABLE.

♥

I AM NOT OTHER PEOPLE'S PERCEPTION OF ME.

♥

MY HAPPINESS IS NOT DEPENDENT ON OTHERS.

♥

I APPROACH NEGATIVE PEOPLE WITH KINDNESS AND EMPATHY.

SPRINKLE

CAPSIZE

SPLASHING

PUDDLE

SEASON

Date: _____

Do not allow their praises to control you...

Date: _____

...or their opinions to make you lose control.

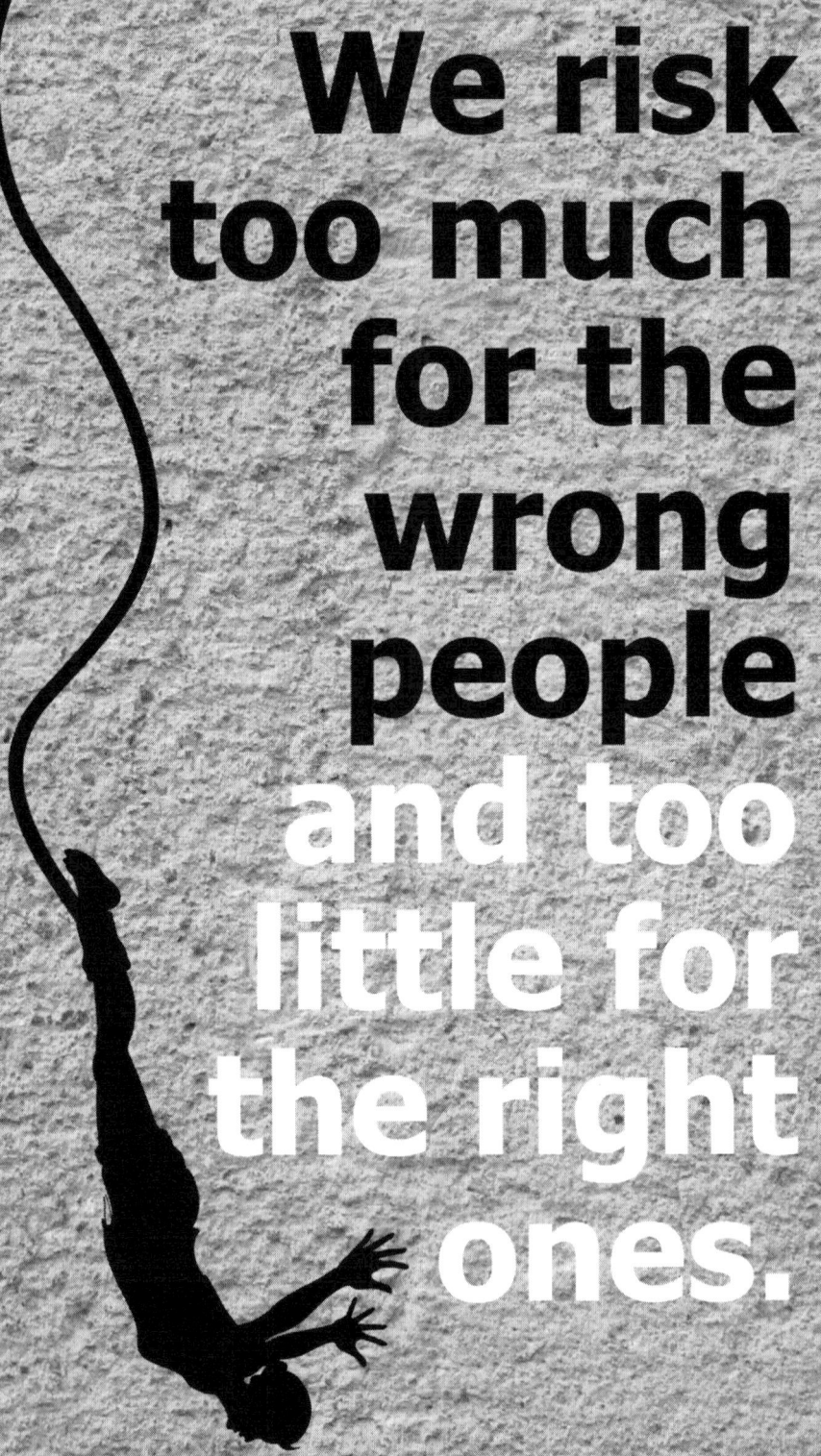

Date: _____

POETRY PROMPT

You must risk your heart to catch love.

Date: _____

What I want...

What I am willing to risk to get it...

There are no guarantees in finding a perfect partner but you can learn to spot habits and behaviors in how you make choices.

What are some characteristics of the wrong partner for you?

What are some characteristics of the right partner for you?

What can you do to make better choices before taking risks with a new partner?

Date: _____

Date: _____

You are a great catch...

Date: _____

... that has fallen into the wrong arms.

Today I will risk it all for my dreams.

♥

I am bold and trust the journey.

♥

Fear does not control me.

♥

There is nothing I can not do if I work at it.

♥

I trust my heart and head to make good decisions.

♥

I am willing to stand up for what I believe in and I believe in me.

JUMP SQUEEZE
WHISPER
FLYING FACE

5

Date: _____

Broken hearts can still love...

Date: _____

... and broken people are still lovable.

Women like her are only hard to love by men who believe LOVE is just a word.

Some bridges are better left burned. Some love stories are better off as ashes.

Date: _____

Make a list of what "love" means to you.

This is a list of what you need to look for in relationships. To accept less than this is to sell yourself short. You deserve more from you.

Date: _____

What things do you do to show love?

How do you think those actions are received by your partner?

What might you need to work on to be better at showing love?

Date: _____

Date: _____

You are only hard to love...

Date: _____

... to those who find walking away easy.

I SEE LOVE. I AM LOVE.
I DESERVE LOVE.

♥

THERE IS ROOM IN MY LIFE FOR REAL LOVE.

♥

I DESERVE A "GOOSEBUMPS" KIND OF RELATIONSHIP.

♥

I WILL BE THE PARTNER THAT I NEED MY PARTNER TO BE.

♥

I AM PREPARED FOR A HEALTHY RELATIONSHIP.

♥

I AM NOT UNLOVABLE. I AM MADE OF LOVE.

TRANSFER   **WORD**
          BEAUTIFUL
DEGREE   **COLLECTION**

5

Date: _____

She wants to be loved with an honest tongue...

Date: _____

...devoted heart, and exclusive eyes.

NOTHING ORDINARY
IS MEANT FOR YOU

There is nothing more unfair to you than convincing yourself that it is okay to accept anything short of extraordinary.

POETRY PROMPT

Being extraordinary isn't an accident that just happens… and it doesn't come naturally to most.

Date: _____

Date: _____

What does being extraordinary mean to you?

_____
_____
_____
_____

Who do you look up to as extraordinary?

_____
_____
_____
_____

Why? What makes them so extraordinary?

_____
_____
_____
_____

What things —big or small— can you do be more extraordinary than you already are?

- Make eye contact & say hello to strangers
- Donate time to charity
- Teach what you've learned

#goals

Date: _____

Date: _____

You are too powerful to be a slave of acceptance.

Date: _____

The love you deserve is meant to know forever.

I DESERVE AN EXTRAORDINARY LIFE.

♥

I AM DOING A GREAT JOB.

♥

I AM OPEN TO THE POSSIBILITIES IN FRONT OF ME.

♥

I AM GRATEFUL FOR THE POSITIVE THINGS IN MY LIFE.

♥

I AM DARING TO ASK FOR MORE BECAUSE I DESERVE IT.

♥

I AM GIVING MYSELF THE LOVE THAT I NEED.

DIFFERENT   **SPEED**   **TRANSFER**
AMAZING   **GLIDE**

5

Date: _____

You deserve to be with someone who...

Date: _____

...searches for the beautiful things in you.

I cannot tell you what burdens she carries, but I can tell that they are **TOO HEAVY** for ONE person to carry.

Date: _____

POETRY PROMPT

Do you ask for help or support when you need it? Why or why not?

Write an open letter to your future self about the burdens you are currently carrying and how you are managing them.

Maybe writing this helped get some things off your chest. Or maybe you just felt better about coming up with some plans on lightening your load.
Either way, be mindful of when to ask for help.
You don't need to do it alone.

Date: _____

Date: _____

Don't let what you are going through today...

Date: _____

...steal tomorrow's beauty.

I ACCEPT MY LIMITATIONS.

♥

I APPRECIATE GENUINE OFFERS OF HELP FROM THOSE WHO CARE ABOUT ME.

♥

I DO NOT NEED TO TAKE ON MORE THAN I CAN HANDLE.

♥

I AM ALLOWED TO SAY NO.

♥

I AM STRONG, EVEN WHEN I DON'T FEEL IT.

♥

NEGATIVITY IS A BURDEN I REFUSE TO CARRY.

LIGHT　　　　　　　　　　**SHIFT**

　　　　　　HELP

ORGANIC　　　　　　　　**GLOBE**

5

Date: _____

Don't let the small losses...

Date: _____

... keep you from the win that matters.

THEY CAN'T BREAK YOU.

They don't have the power to break **FIGHTERS**
You can only scar **WARRIORS**;
CONQUERORS are meant to overcome.

Whatever it is that is trying to hold you under does not have enough strength to keep you down.

Only you carry such power.

Date: _____

Do not hide from your weaknesses; learn them, find out what causes them, and pay close attention to them…

Make a list of your weaknesses.

Date: _____

….because when you become aware of them, you become capable of changing them.

What things can you do to change those weaknesses into strengths?

Date: _____

Remember, you are winning...

Date: _____

... even when there aren't enough people cheering!

I AM STRONGER THAN MY BIGGEST FEARS.

♥

I AM POWERFUL.

♥

I AM UNSTOPPABLE AND I NEVER GIVE UP.

♥

I CAN PERSIST EVEN WHEN TIMES ARE CHALLENGING.

♥

IT IS OKAY TO PUT MYSELF FIRST AND FIGHT FOR WHAT I NEED.

♥

OBSTACLES ARE TEMPORARY WHEN I CONFRONT THEM WITH EYES WIDE OPEN.

SCAR   FAMILIAR
        BRUISED
RANDOM   WISH

5

Date: _____

Her defensive ways are safety checks...

Date: _____

... for those trying to enter her heart.

There is nothing wrong with being an **OLD SOUL**

waiting on **NEW L♥VE.**

You don't need to find closure to find happiness again, you need to find reasons to start a new chapter, and put down that old book.

Here is one reason:
you deserve to be happy.

Date: _____

 Write a letter to an old love about your need to move forward.

Date: _____

Moving on is always challenging whether your relationship ended mutually, badly, or even through the death of your soulmate. It's going to be work to move on but you can do it.

And... I promise that even though it may be difficult at times, it will be worth your efforts.

Date: _____

Young love is beautiful...

Date: _____

...but old love is real.

I am worthy of love.

♥

The best part of my life is just beginning.

♥

There is room in my life for someone new to love.

♥

I complete me.

♥

Everything is happening as it should.

♥

I appreciate the healing process.

BENCH   DRINK
         WORDS
FOREVER   BEGINNING

5

Date: _____

Self-love isn't something we do for a season...

Date: _____

... it's a lifetime journey.

Final Words from Pierre

I'm so proud of you!

You made it to the end of this journal. I hope the bottled emotions were emptied in here. I hope this lead to a lot of self-reflection and inspiration to keep traveling your path to comfortably standing in your truth.

Writing, to me, has always been therapeutic - a way to give a voice to thoughts you don't care to be heard. There is freedom in it. I hope you at least tasted a little bit of that in this journal. Keep giving a pen to your mind and letting the trapped words find their way out.

— Pierre

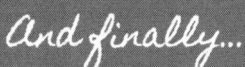

Many of the 19 quote in this book can be purchased as wall art, mugs, t-shirts, and other merchandise at pierrejeanty.com

Use code **JOURNAL20** for 20% off.

Look for Pierre Jeanty on these social platforms